FRANKLIN PARK PUBLIC LIBRARY

FRANKLIN PARK, IL.

Each borrower is held responsible for all library material drawn on his card and for fines accruing on the same. No material will be issued until such fine has been paid.

All injuries to library material beyond reasonable wear and all losses shall be made good to the satisfaction of the Library

Replacement costs will be
billed after 42 days overdue.

YOU TAKE A BATH

By DAVID I. A. MASON

Illustrated by DAN WIDDOWSON

CANTATA LEARNING

MANKATO, MINNESOTA

WWW.CANTATALEARNING.COM

CANTATA
LEARNING
MANKATO, MINNESOTA

Published by Cantata Learning
1710 Roe Crest Drive
North Mankato, MN 56003
www.cantatalearning.com

Library of Congress Control Number: 2014957040
978-1-63290-292-4 (hardcover/CD)
978-1-63290-444-7 (paperback/CD)
978-1-63290-486-7 (paperback)

You Take a Bath by David I. A. Mason
Illustrated by Dan Widdowson

Book design, Tim Palin Creative
Editorial direction, Flat Sole Studio
Executive musical production and direction, Elizabeth Draper
Music arranged and produced by Mark Oblinger

Printed in the United States of America.

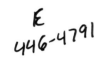

VISIT
WWW.CANTATALEARNING.COM/ACCESS-OUR-MUSIC
TO SING ALONG TO THE SONG

Having a clean body helps keep you **healthy**. During each day, **germs** can get on your face, hands, and body. Germs can make you sick. Taking a bath washes germs away. Being clean also makes you feel and smell good.

Now turn the page, and sing along.

You just got home from playing tag.

You're tired. You're **sweaty**.

And you're starting to **drag**.

You had a lot of fun playing in the dirt.

You're covered in mud. It's even under your shirt!

You know what
you have to do!

You take a bath.
What do you do?

You take a bath!

Scrub your ears and neck and face.

And **rinse** yourself all over the place.

Yeah, take a bath.

You just finished dinner with your mom and dad.

It was the messiest meal you've ever had.

The need to get clean is oh so clear.

You have macaroni and cheese in your ear.

You know what
you have to do!

You take a bath.

What do you do?

You take a bath!

Scrub your ears and neck and face.
And rinse yourself all over the place.

Yeah, take a bath.

It's the end of the day, and you're feeling grimy.

Your hair's a bit stinky, your toes a bit slimy.

During the day, germs found their way onto your skin.
Get some soap. Fill the tub. Ready to jump in?

You know what
you have to do!

You take a bath.
What do you do?

You take a bath!

Scrub your ears and neck and face.

And rinse yourself all over the place.

Yeah, take a bath.

Water, soap. Wash, rinse.

Water, soap. Wash, rinse.

Water, soap. Wash, rinse.

You know what
you have to do!

You take a bath.
What do you do?

You take a bath!

Wash yourself from head to toe.

And surely everyone
will know you took a bath!

SONG LYRICS
You Take a Bath

You just got home from playing
tag.
You're tired. You're sweaty.
And you're starting to drag.

You had a lot of fun playing in
the dirt.
You're covered in mud. It's even
under your shirt!

You know what
you have to do!

You take a bath.
What do you do?

You take a bath!

Scrub your ears and neck and
face.
And rinse yourself all over the
place.

Yeah, take a bath.

You just finished dinner with
your mom and dad.
It was the messiest meal you've
ever had.

The need to get clean is oh so
clear.
You have macaroni and cheese
in your ear.

You know what
you have to do!

You take a bath.
What do you do?

You take a bath!

Scrub your ears and neck and
face.
And rinse yourself all over the
place.

Yeah, take a bath.

It's the end of the day, and you're
feeling grimy.
Your hair's a bit stinky, your toes
a bit slimy.

During the day, germs found
their way onto your skin.
Get some soap. Fill the tub.
Ready to jump in?

You know what
you have to do!

You take a bath.
What do you do?

You take a bath!

Scrub your ears and neck and
face.
And rinse yourself all over the
place.

Yeah, take a bath.

Water, soap. Wash, rinse.
Water, soap. Wash, rinse.
Water, soap. Wash, rinse.

You know what
you have to do!

You take a bath.
What do you do?

You take a bath!

Wash yourself from head to toe.
And surely everyone will know.

You took a bath!

Boogie Woogie
Mark Oblinger

You Take a Bath

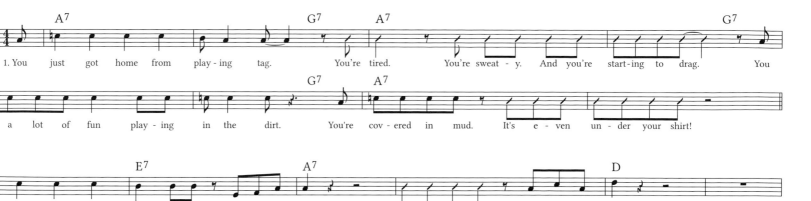

Verse

1. You just got home from play-ing tag. You're tired. You're sweat-y. And you're start-ing to drag. You had a lot of fun play-ing in the dirt. You're cov-ered in mud. It's e-ven un-der your shirt!

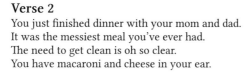

Chorus

You know what you have to do! You take a bath. What do you do? You take a bath! Scrub your ears and neck and face. And rinse your-self all o-ver the place. Yeah, take a bath.

Verse 2

You just finished dinner with your mom and dad.
It was the messiest meal you've ever had.
The need to get clean is oh so clear.
You have macaroni and cheese in your ear.

Chorus

You know what you have to do!
You take a bath. What do you do? You take a bath!
Scrub your ears and neck and face.
And rinse yourself all over the place. Yeah, take a bath.

Bridge

It's the end of the day, and you're feel-ing grim-y. Your hair's a bit stink-y, your toes a bit slim-y. Dur-ing the day, germs found their way on-to your skin. Get some soap. Fill the tub. Read-y to jump in?

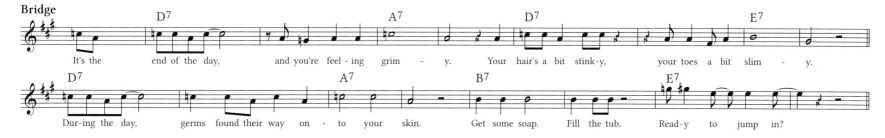

Chorus

You know what you have to do!
You take a bath. What do you do? You take a bath!
Scrub your ears and neck and face.
And rinse yourself all over the place. Yeah, take a bath.

Spoken

Water, soap. Wash, rinse.
Water, soap. Wash, rinse.
Water, soap. Wash, rinse.

Chorus

You know what you have to do!
You take a bath. What do you do? You take a bath!
Wash yourself from head to toe.
And surely everyone will know you took a bath!

GLOSSARY

drag—to be tired and move slowly

germs—tiny living things that can cause illness

healthy—fit and well, not sick

rinse: to wash away with clean water

sweaty—wet with the perspiration that forms on skin when you are hot or nervous

GUIDED READING ACTIVITIES

1. When do you usually take a bath? Why is it important to take a bath?

2. Draw a picture of a time when you were really dirty and needed to take a bath. What were you doing that made you so dirty?

3. What did the characters in this book do to get ready for a bath? What steps did they do to get clean?

TO LEARN MORE

Anderson, Peggy Perry. *To the Tub*. Boston: Sandpiper, 2012.

Dahl, Michael. *Pig Takes a Bath*. Mankato, MN: Picture Window Books, 2010.

Gleisner, Jenna Lee. *My Body Needs to Be Clean*. Mankato, MN: Amicus High Interest, 2015.

Tourville, Amanda Doering. *Go Wash Up: Keeping Clean*. Minneapolis: Picture Window Books, 2009.

9863022